THE DISCIPLE

THE DISCIPLE
A JOURNEY WITH GOD

DFD 2.4 a study of how to be like Christ

NAVPRESS

Discipleship Inside Out™

NavPress is the publishing ministry of The Navigators, an international
Christian organization and leader in personal spiritual development.
NavPress is committed to helping people grow spiritually and enjoy lives
of meaning and hope through personal and group resources that are
biblically rooted, culturally relevant, and highly practical.

For a free catalog go to www.NavPress.com
or call 1.800.366.7788 in the United States or 1.800.839.4769 in Canada.

TH1NK and the TH1NK logo are registered trademarks of NavPress. Absence of ® in
connection with marks of NavPress or other parties does not indicate an absence of
registration of those marks.

ISBN 978-1-57683-639-2

Cover design by BURNKIT
Creative Team: Eric Johnson, Gabe Filkey, Rachelle Gardner, Kathy Mosier,
    Pat Reinheimer

Unless otherwise identified, all Scripture quotations in this publication are taken from the
HOLY BIBLE: NEW INTERNATIONAL VERSION® (NIV®). Copyright © 1973, 1978,
1984 by International Bible Society. Used by permission of Zondervan Publishing House.
All rights reserved. Additional version used is *THE MESSAGE* (MSG). Copyright © 1993,
1994, 1995, 1996, 2000, 2001, 2002. Used by permission of NavPress Publishing Group.

Printed in the United States of America

5 6 7 8 9 10 / 14 13 12 11

INTRODUCTION

No turning back.

If you don't love Christ as much as you love your life as it currently is, now would be a good time to stop reading this book. There, you heard it here first. You can't go into Discipleship halfway. To paraphrase Revelation 3:16, "Be hot or cold," God said. "The room temperature stuff makes Me throw up." Look it up. He really did say it.

Being a Disciple is about being hot. Really hot. When Jesus called His first Disciples, He said, "Follow Me." Twelve people answered His call. The Bible says Peter immediately quit what he was doing to begin his Discipleship. As a fisherman, he literally dropped his nets to follow Christ. Jesus didn't allow people who were too busy "doing life" or who wanted to "wait a few years" to be His Disciples, harsh as that might sound. They had a room temperature faith.

Discipleship is a lifelong process, not some fad or ephemeral trend. There's no such thing as a layaway faith—the someday-I'll-get-serious-about-God type of faith. Either you are into it heart, soul, and mind—"on fire" for Christ—or you're not.

Loving God and deciding to follow Him takes life out of your control and puts it into God's hands. *Have plans for your life?* Ditch them, because being a Disciple will lead you to people, places, and experiences you've never even dreamed of.

If this type of life excites you, you may already have heard the call from Christ: "Follow Me. Go into all the world and tell people about Me. Love Me above everything else." If you're ready to "drop your nets" and follow Christ, you've come to the right place.

CHAPTER 1

DISCIPLE DEFINED

A Disciple is a learner, an apprentice. But when you're a Disciple of Christ, there's no graduation. A Disciple's education never ends because there's always so much more to learn. And while it's true that some lessons can be learned once, many others will be learned again and again to increasingly greater levels of proficiency.

However, more important than the types of lessons we encounter is what we learn about God and His ways. God is beyond anything we could ever just "figure out." That's why it takes a lifetime and an eternity to fully appreciate and enjoy how awe-inspiring He is. The more we as Disciples learn about our Master, the more we realize how perfect He is—the more breathtakingly complex and beautiful He becomes.

That's what makes God who He is and why He is worth our whole life. Fortunately, the Father has given us the Holy Spirit to help us become more like Him. As you set out to be a Disciple, depend on God's Spirit to teach you, lead you, and speak to you—to help you begin to know God better. Embrace your learner status and discover why it's so exciting to get to know God, even if it's just in little bits and pieces at a time.

1. You already know that Jesus had twelve Disciples. But those were only the first twelve. Since then, millions of people have answered the call to follow Christ—to be His Disciples. Read what Jesus said about the requirements of being a Disciple in Luke 14:25-27 and then answer the following questions.

a. What two things did Jesus say we must do if we are to be His Disciples?

b. Do we literally have to hate our families or carry a cross? In your own words, explain what these phrases mean.

c. What point was Jesus trying to get across by using such strong language?

2. Look up the following passages from the book of John. Identify some more traits of Christ-Disciples from these verses and decide how your life matches up.

	Trait	**Present in My Life?**
John 8:31:		
John 13:34-35:		
John 15:8:		

*Extra Credit: If one or more of these traits currently aren't present in your life, write down some things you can do to change that.

3. Using the Bible passages from questions 1 and 2, write a brief definition of *Disciple.*

4. Why do you think Jesus' standards for His Disciples are so high?

5. The Disciple is a learner, an apprentice—almost like an intern. Jesus Himself took education seriously, both His own and that of others around Him. What attitude toward instruction should characterize a Disciple (Proverbs 4:13; 12:1)?

6. In 1 Corinthians 14:20, Paul told his readers three things: (1) don't think like little kids, (2) be innocent as babies toward evil, and (3) think critically like adults. How well do you rate in each of these areas? In which area are you the strongest? In which are you the weakest?

7. Go back to Proverbs. Read 11:14 and 24:30-34. What do these verses say about people who lack understanding?

COST/BENEFIT ANALYSIS

Being a Disciple isn't free. As you saw earlier, Jesus has high expectations for people who think they want to walk in His steps.

8. Revisit Luke 14; this time read 14:28-32. Jesus told a couple of short stories to illustrate what Discipleship takes.

   a. What does Jesus want His Disciples to have in the back of their minds as they set out to Journey with Him?

   b. Why do you suppose Jesus has to remind us of this fact?

   c. In what ways are you making sure that you'll be able to finish what you started?

9. Some people don't consider the costs of Discipleship. In Luke 9:57-62, Jesus met some people who *thought* they wanted to follow the Master.

    a. What stopped them?

    b. How can you make sure you don't end up like one of these people who chickened out?

10. Stay in Luke 9 and look back at verses 23 and 24. Again, Jesus told His would-be Disciples to carry their cross—daily. Using the four phrases below, write a paragraph explaining Jesus' main point in this passage. In your paragraph, try to explain how all of these statements are essential to your Journey with God.

    Deny yourself.   **Take up your cross.**
    Follow Christ.   **Lose your life to find it.**

11. Read Romans 12:1-2. How would you explain the "living sacrifice" concept? How is it relevant to a life of Discipleship?

> He is no fool who gives up what he cannot keep to
> gain what he cannot lose.
>
> —JIM ELLIOT, martyr and missionary in the Amazon*

12. In prayer, ask God what kind of cross He wants you to carry every day. Talk honestly to God about what you see as the costs of being a Disciple. Ask Him to help you see the benefits. Write down some ways you can keep yourself focused on the benefits rather than the costs.

---

* Elisabeth Elliot, ed., *The Journals of Jim Elliot* (Old Tappan, N. J.: Revell, 1978), p. 174.

13. It's easier to have all the right answers than it is to live them out. And it's easier to live them out than it is to live them out *with the right motives*. But motives count. (See 1 Corinthians 13 for more on this subject.) What is the only genuine motive for being a Disciple (1 John 4:10-12)?

*Extra Credit: What are some common wrong motives people might have for following Christ? Examine your life for faulty motives — which, by the way, are any motives that don't center around your love and enjoyment of Christ.

14. As a follow-up to this passage, look at Jesus' interaction with Peter in John 21:15-19. Three times, the Master asked Peter if he loved Him. Notice that it was only *after* Peter affirmed his love that Jesus asked Peter to do anything. Love of Christ is the motive for Discipleship. Read this passage a couple of times and put yourself in Peter's shoes. How do you think he felt? How would you respond if Jesus asked you these questions face-to-face?

WHAT DISCIPLES ARE LIKE

15. In 2 Timothy 2:3-6, Paul compared the Disciple of Christ to three types of people: a soldier, an athlete, and a farmer. Read the passage. Then pick one of these analogies and describe how it relates to your life as a Disciple.

16. One thing Disciples aren't is lazy. Yet it's so easy to cover up behind a facade of busyness. Read Hebrews 6:11-12 and answer the following questions.

a. What is diligence?

b. What is the difference between relaxation and laziness?

c. According to this passage, why are Disciples diligent instead of lazy? (Hint: Again, think about the true motive of Discipleship.)

17. Much of your commitment to Discipleship revolves around an attitude you do or don't have. Explain how your outlook on life compares to that described in Philippians 3:10-15.

18. Flip ahead to the next book and read Colossians 3:17. Compare Paul's advice/command in this verse with the passage from question 17. How do the two passages go together?

19. Why do our attitudes and motives toward God and others—our "heart"—matter so much (Proverbs 6:12-19)?

20. *Carpe Discipleship.* *Discipline* and *Disciple* stem from the same root word in Latin, *discipere.* The prefix *dis* means "apart" and *capere* means "to take or seize." Together, they mean "to seize an idea, take it apart, and make it yours"—make it part of you. List some areas of your life in which you want to exercise greater discipline and diligence. (This can be anything from making a plan to read the Bible, to watching less TV, to striving to be more honest at school.)

SUMMARY

Look back over your answers to the questions in this chapter.
Summarize what it means to be a Disciple.

CHAPTER 2

USING WHAT GOD GIVES US

Some gifts are universal—like time, for example. Every person is given the gift of twenty-four hours each day to live for God's glory. That doesn't change as long as we are alive. But some gifts are unique. Your family might own a jet and a 5,000-square-foot "retreat" in Vail; another Disciple might be an AIDS orphan from a developing country. Or, you might have musical talent; another Disciple might speak persuasively in front of large crowds. You get the picture.

The apostle Paul said, "Whatever you do, do it all for the glory of God" (1 Corinthians 10:31). As you might remember from *The Faith*, the third book in the DFD 2.0 series, God in His sovereignty has bestowed each of His children with his or her own unique function in the body of Christ. Each person has gifts, resources, and abilities to use. But across the board, one thing is the same: Everybody is to use them to bring glory to God. It's something called stewardship.

1. Stewardship is making the most of what God has entrusted to us—time, money, and talents. In 1 Corinthians 4:2, Paul told his readers that they must "prove faithful." In what ways do you prove yourself faithful with your resources?

2. The book of Proverbs is full of little quips and one-liners about being responsible with our resources and energy. Try to find one such passage and tell how it relates to your life. (Hint: If you can't find one, try Proverbs 3:9-10.)

3. Proverbs isn't the only place where we can read about stewardship. In Matthew 25:14-30, Jesus told His Disciples a story about what it means to use everything we are and everything we have for God's glory. Read this passage and in a short paragraph, summarize its main point for someone who is a new follower of Christ.

TIME

4. How we use our time is one of the best indicators of our real heart for God. Talk is nothing compared to the richness of dedicated, Christ-centered action. Read Matthew 6:25-34.

a. List one or two things from this passage that struck you. What caught your attention?

b. Reread verse 33. Why do you think Jesus wants His Disciples to first seek God's kingdom and righteousness—even before our own food and clothing?

c. Think about your own life; look at your actions and habits. What do you seek first? What's most important to you?

5. Timothy was a young person who proved himself a faithful and diligent steward. Paul mentored Timothy and encouraged him to keep doing the right things. How is Paul's advice in 1 Timothy 4:12-16 applicable to your own life? What practical steps can you take to be a modern-day Timothy?

6. Reading the Bible, praying, going to church—these aren't the only ways we can show that we are Disciples of Christ. Everything we do (homework, sports, art, working at Target) is an opportunity and a

responsibility to live for God's glory. In fact, the work we do is a very important part of Discipleship. Read 2 Thessalonians 3:7-13.

a. What is the difference between working hard and being a busybody?

b. Why do you think God wants His Disciples to work hard at what they do?

7. What are your priorities? In the blanks on the left side, number the following items as they currently exist in your life (1 as the most important thing and 5 as the least important). In the blanks on the right side, number them as you think God would have them exist in your life.

My Current Priority   **God's Priority**

___   Job (your present job; your future career)   ___

___   God (loving Him; being His Disciple and child)   ___

___   Family   ___
         (your mom, dad, and siblings; your future family)

___   Ministry (worship; telling others about Christ)   ___

___   Other (movies; sports; hobbies; hanging out)   ___

8. Compare the two lists of priorities.

    a. What differences do you notice, if any?

    b. If there are differences, how can you change your day-to-day life to make God's priorities your priorities?

    c. Step back to the beginning. Why would a person want to make God a priority in the first place?

9. How should a Disciple use his or her time? Read Ephesians 5:15-21 and Colossians 4:2,5-6 and write down three or four practical ideas you can apply to make the most of every moment you have. Evaluate how relevant each item is to your life.

THE CRAZY CONCEPT OF GIVING OUR MONEY AWAY

10. As Disciples, we can't let ourselves get carried away by the desire for money and the things money can provide. Read 1 Timothy 6:9-10. Do you agree that the "love of money is a root of all kinds of evil"? Explain your answer.

11. Now read the verses that directly follow that passage: 1 Timothy 6:11-12. According to these verses, how can you as a Disciple "fight the good fight"? What does this look like in your life?

12. Money is important to real life, and it's an important topic in the Bible. Here are five more passages that are related to our attitude and use of money. Read all five. Then choose *one* and explain in your own words how it applies to your view of money (Proverbs 20:10; Proverbs 22:7; Luke 12:15; Luke 16:11; Ephesians 4:28).

13. In 2 Corinthians 9, Paul spelled out several principles relating to a Disciple's view of money—in general that it really is a privilege to be able to give a little or a lot of it away for God's purposes. In the space below, record what you discover in each of the following verses. (You may want to read the entire chapter to understand the context.)

Verse 6:

Verse 7:

Verse 8:

Verse 11:

Verse 12:

Verse 13:

14. Jesus also spoke about money issues. He took advantage of one opportunity in particular to turn our view of wealth upside down. Read about this instance in Mark 12:41-44. As far as our giving to Him is concerned, what is most important to God?

*Extra Credit: Among a myriad of motives and incentives, giving requires a conscious choice. The best way to get into a habit of giving is to make a plan. Grab a piece of paper and follow these steps to create a plan:

1. Decide what percentage of your income you want to give back to God. Many people use the "tithe" (10 percent) as a standard; some call that a minimum. Wherever you are on this issue, ask God what percentage He wants you to give, listen to Him, and stick with it.

2. When you get paid, set aside that money first—before you use it to go to the movies, pay the bills, or buy any number of other wants or needs.

3. This is the fun part: Pray about where God would like you to give this money. Maybe He wants you to support a certain missionary, give some to your church, help orphans in Africa, or whatever. Pray for God's direction and really learn how to have *fun* by offering back a portion of your money to God.

Write out your plan and put it somewhere you can always see it. Maybe you can laminate it and keep it in your wallet or purse as a constant reminder that God is the source of all your resources; giving some back to Him is just one way to thank and worship Him for His goodness.*

---

*For more information about the joys of giving your money away, you might want to read *The Treasure Principle* by Randy Alcorn.

TALENTS, INTERESTS, AND ABILITIES

15. As you've read in previous DFD 2.0 books, God has charged and equipped each person to serve Him with his or her unique talents, interests, and abilities. As a review, read 1 Peter 4:10-11. How are Disciples supposed to use their gifts?

16. Because God has gifted each person differently, there are opportunities for our human nature to get the best of us, like when we're jealous or judgmental. We might think, *I wish I had those gifts,* or *That person can't do anything.* Find Romans 12:3-8.

a. List some of the different gifts God gives to His Disciples (verses 6-8).

b. How are we supposed to think about our talents in relation to the abilities of others (verse 3)?

c. Paul used the human body as an analogy for the symbiotic relationship all believers have with one another. Do you think this is a realistic picture of how we work together? Why or why not?

17. One more time: The Father designed people—giving them their own looks, health, voice, ideas, talents, and character traits. And there's a reason for it: He wants us to honor Him through what we have. *He loves us.* Because He loves us, we love Him. Because we love Him, we as His Disciples want to make the most of the resources He has given us. Thinking about your own life, write down some area in which God has gifted you and how you might be able to use that gift to serve and worship Him.

TAKE A SHOWER, FOR THE LOVE OF GOD

18. You might think this goes without saying, but we need to take care of our bodies. If we are careless about our bodies—if we overeat, don't shower, refuse to brush our teeth—we won't be able to honor God effectively. (We'll be too busy putting ointment on our open sores and scratching our lice to even pray.) With that mental picture in mind, read 1 Corinthians 6:19-20. What does it mean that your body is a "temple of the Holy Spirit"?

19. Turn back to Romans 12 and read verse 1. What does this verse tell us to do with our bodies, and how do we make that happen?

20. It's much easier to pray and worship God when we don't have a 104-degree fever and when we have fully functioning lungs (although we must remember that God can use an illness for His glory). So is it acceptable to pray about staying healthy (3 John 2)? Explain your answer.

21. You've seen the news: Kids are getting . . . um, shall we say . . . *larger,* diabetes is on the rise, people aren't exercising enough. As a Disciple in charge of God's temple (your body), identify any problems you might have in the following four practical areas. Write down some ideas for improvement.

a. Eating right:

b. Exercising regularly:

c. Getting enough sleep:

d. Refusing bad habits (such as sleeping around, getting drunk, and the like):

SUMMARY

Write a summary of this chapter. Include an answer to this question: What is your *major* motivation for being a steward of your time, money, abilities, and body?

CHAPTER 3

BEING AN AMBASSADOR

Here's some good news or bad news, depending on how you look at it: You, as a Disciple, are the living embodiment of Christ to the world. Everywhere you go and in everything you do, you take Christ's name with you. If you walk into a nudie video store, Christ goes with you. If you stink, Christ stinks. If you eat like a glutton, Christ eats like a glutton.

But if you show kindness, Christ shows kindness. If you are a selfless servant, Christ is a selfless servant.

This is what Paul called being an ambassador for Christ (2 Corinthians 5:20). It's a very tall order, but it is central to our Discipleship. It's a great analogy. Ambassadors live in foreign countries and represent the best interests, opinions, and ways of their leader back home. Considering that the true home of Disciples is God's kingdom, we represent our King and His power to a world that otherwise has no idea He even exists.

Because part of being a Disciple is being an ambassador, we need to realize that our lives will be scrutinized and picked apart. And because actions speak louder than words—much louder, in fact—it pays to remember often that we represent not only ourselves but also our God by the way we live. Many people won't initially read the Bible, but they will "read" our lifestyles and actions.

WORLDVIEW

1. Being a Disciple is global. To paraphrase some of Jesus' final instructions, "Go everywhere! Tell everyone in every country about Me and show them how to be Disciples!" (Matthew 28:19-20). Obviously, it was important to Jesus that all people have an opportunity to know Him and love Him as their Master and Savior. As a jumping-off point, rate from 1 to 10 your passion and heart to share the gospel with others—here, there, and everywhere.

1	2	3	4	5	6	7	8	9	10
(weak)									(strong)

2. There's a reason Disciples must heed Jesus' advice and have a heart for their world. Read Paul's words in Romans 10:14-18.

a. Write down the four questions Paul posed and answer each one.

●

●

●

●

b. So what? How does this apply to your life? (Hint: See verse 15.)

c. Now look at verse 17. How does anyone begin to possess faith?

3. One way we are able to bring God's message to others is by telling our personal stories. Whose "beautiful feet" brought you the good news about Jesus? Write a short paragraph explaining how you first heard about Christ and committed your life to God.

4. John 3:16 is almost cliché, which is a shame because the verse is so powerful. In just a few lines, it tells us so much about a God—a Father—who loves us. Read the verse a few times and answer these two questions: Why is God's world vision so important? How can we begin to see the world like God sees it?

> World Vision is getting on your heart what is on God's
> heart—the world.
>
> —DAWSON TROTMAN*

5. Jesus often talked about sending His Disciples throughout the
world. In fact, He did send the original twelve Disciples out—three
times, including one time recorded in Acts 1:8. All of this sending
demands this question: Why doesn't He just appear to each person
Himself and save them, when it's definitely within His power to do
so? Read these passages and try to explain why God wants us to be
His witnesses to others: Mark 16:15; John 17:18; John 20:21; Acts 1:8.

6. Sometimes people wanted to follow Jesus, but when He asked
them to see the world the way He saw it—to share their lives and
resources with others—they couldn't do it (Matthew 9:37-38). Why
do you think it is so difficult to share Christ's heart and His vision for
the world?

7. As Disciples, we strive to share God's love with a broken world
because without Christ, there is no eternal hope. What fate awaits
those who reject the gospel of Christ (2 Thessalonians 1:8-9;
Revelation 20:12,15)?

*Taken from *Growing in Discipleship* (Colorado Springs, Colo.: NavPress, 1980), p. 39.

GET TO KNOW YOUR WORLD

The total world population is approximately 6,336,933,481 and growing (literally) every second.* What do you know about these people? How can one person make a difference?

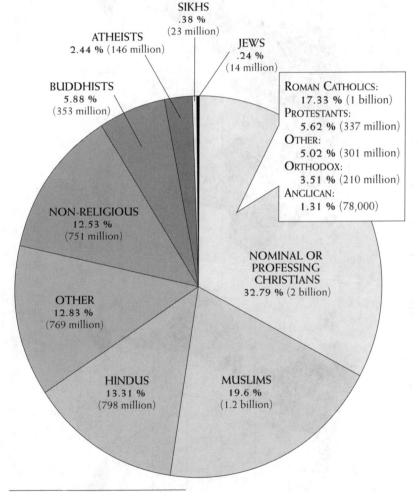

*Data taken from the U.S. Census Bureau, International Programs Center, http://www.census.gov/main/www/popclock.html (accessed December 19, 2003).

Pie Chart Source: *The World Factbook,* "People," http://www.odci.gov/cia/ publications/factbook/geos/xx.html#people (accessed February 5, 2004).

"God was reconciling the world to himself in Christ." (2 Corinthians 5:19)

WORLD POPULATION
BY AREA

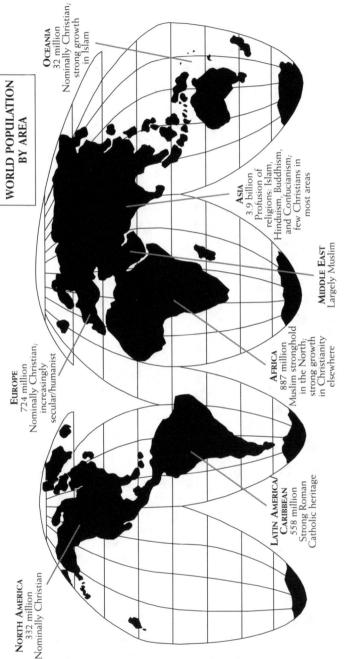

EUROPE
724 million
Nominally Christian;
increasingly
secular/humanist

OCEANIA
32 million
Nominally Christian;
strong growth
in Islam

ASIA
3.9 billion
Profusion of
religions: Islam,
Hinduism, Buddhism,
and Confucianism;
few Christians in
most areas

MIDDLE EAST
Largely Muslim

AFRICA
887 million
Muslim stronghold
in the North;
strong growth
in Christianity
elsewhere

**LATIN AMERICA/
CARIBBEAN**
558 million
Strong Roman
Catholic heritage

NORTH AMERICA
332 million
Nominally Christian

"The field is the world." (Matthew 13:38)

Source: Population Division of the Department of Economic and Social Affairs of the United Nations Secretariat, *World Population Prospects: The 2002 Revision* and *Urbanization Prospects: The 2001 Revision.*

Even if you aren't a missionary in another country, you can still have an impact if you hold true to God's world vision and love others as God loves us. But remember, it all begins with where you are today. Here are a few ideas of how you can make a difference:

- Use a map or a book such as *Operation World* to pray for various countries around the world. Pray that the people living there would hear about Christ's message.
- Get to know missionaries. Learn about their work. Pray for them. Support them financially.
- Read biographies of missionaries. Get inspired by what God has done and is doing through other Disciples' lives.
- Go on a mission trip yourself. Ask God to lead you and give you a heart for sharing His love with others around the world.
- Don't forget to look around you in your community for opportunities to talk about how Christ has changed your life.

BEING AN AMBASSADOR

8. The U.S. State Department (www.state.gov) is in charge of sending Americans to other countries to represent the United States—to explain the U.S.'s stance on certain policy issues and to promote the U.S.'s best interests. In 2 Corinthians 5:20-21, Paul used the term *ambassador* to describe our role for Christ in this world. In what ways do you think this is or isn't a valid comparison?

9. Philippians 2:14-16 gives an "ambassador job description." Read the passage and then give yourself a grade on each of the four characteristics that follow. (You can use A, B, C, D, and F like you are given in school.)

Task	**Grade**
Does not complain or argue	_____
Is blameless and pure	_____
Shines like a star	_____
Holds out the word of life	_____

a. Which is your weakest area?

b. What steps can you take to improve your ambassador candidacy?

10. Read 1 Peter 1:17 and 2:11. These verses augment the ambassador comparison.

a. In what ways are we "aliens" in this world?

b. If we are aliens, where is our homeland?

c. How do we represent our King and our King's message in this foreign country?

ALL THINGS TO ALL PEOPLE

As Disciples, we live out our relationship with Christ and represent God to all people, not just to a select few. While we go about our day-to-day lives, we show others what it's like to follow Christ. This is the essence of evangelism. The idea is that we can live our lives in such a way as to inspire others to wonder why Christ-followers are different—*different in a good way.*

11. Read 1 Peter 3:15-16. This passage gives Disciples a step-by-step approach for letting others see Christ in their lives.

a. What two things did Peter tell us to do (verse 15)?

-
-

b. Now look at how we should react when others wonder about our lives. List the three ways (verses 15 and 16).

-
-
-

c. Synthesize these concepts. Why is it important not only to do what these verses call us to do, but to do it with the right attitude?

d. What would happen if a Disciple did the first part, but not the second?

12. Turn to Matthew 9:10-12.

a. Who did Jesus seek out to befriend?

b. What can we learn from His example?

c. Who might you seek out—someone you would otherwise have been inclined to ignore?

13. In Acts, we see that Paul did whatever it took to share Christ's message with others. Why did he (and why should we as well) go to such lengths to make contact with those who didn't yet believe in Christ (Acts 20:20-21)?

14. To reach those around him, Paul not only went wherever necessary, but he also communicated with each person in a way he or she could understand. You see, he didn't subscribe to the one-size-fits-all theory of evangelism. That's part of being a loving ambassador and Disciple for Christ. Paul took the time to relate to people and to speak their language so he could effectively share Christ. There's much to learn from his example. Read his words in 1 Corinthians 9:19-23 and answer the following questions.

a. In verse 19, Paul acknowledged that he had the right to be free (including the right not to care about others, perhaps?), but what did he do with that right?

b. Paul became "all things to all men" (verse 22). Why? Was he living a big lie? Did he befriend people out of sleazy self-interest or for another, more noble reason?

c. What kinds of people do you know? Jocks, skaters, brains, cheerleaders? How can you share Christ's unbelievable love and grace with them—without being phony?

15. Think of your friends and acquaintances. In your day-to-day interactions with them, how are you showing them Christ's love and concern for their lives? (Hint: Remember the old cliché—*Actions speak louder than words.* If you don't really love them or care about them, it doesn't matter what you say.)

KNOWING IT ALL WITHOUT BEING A KNOW-IT-ALL

16. If there's one person who knew how to recognize a person's needs, it was Jesus. He saw through people, to the very core of their soul. He knew that all people have an innate need for God, for a Savior, and for the gift of the Holy Spirit. Jesus challenged people to really think about what is most important in life. Read Mark 10:17-22.

a. What did the man want?

b. But Jesus knew what he actually needed. What was it?

c. How did Jesus annihilate this guy's comfort zone?

d. Why did Jesus say what He said? What was the motive behind it?

17. In the last passage, Jesus quoted ancient Scripture to (lovingly) prove His point. Why can this be an effective technique (Hebrews 4:12)?

18. God's Word tells people not only why they need a Savior but how He can be found. Go back to John 3:16. This time read verses 17 and 18 as well. Try to apply all you have learned so far and answer the following questions.

a. What three points summarize the gospel message (verse 16)?

-
-
-

b. Why did God send His Son, Jesus, to the world (verse 17)?

c. How do these verses show us (and others) the importance of Christ?

19. After the Holy Spirit in you has inspired your friends to wonder about Christ and you have given "the reason for the hope that you have" (1 Peter 3:15), you might offer to pray for or with them. Offer them a chance to pray to the Father to accept Christ as Master, Lord, and Savior of their lives. Why do you think this might be an important step for your friends to take?

20. The Bible is great—to the Disciples who believe and to those open to hearing about it. But the Bible is "foolishness to those who are perishing" (1 Corinthians 1:18). So don't be surprised if you encounter fierce opposition to your beliefs. How should you react if someone absolutely doesn't want to hear about your faith in God (2 Timothy 2:23-26)?

Maybe you've already experienced objections to your faith. To help you respond to them, the following list gives some things people say to reject Christ—and some verses that counter those objections.

Objection	**Bible Verses**
"What about those who have never heard the gospel?"	Psalm 19:1; Psalm 97:6; Romans 1:19-20; Acts 14:17
"What about the errors in the Bible?"	Isaiah 55:8-9; 2 Timothy 3:16
"Why do so many educated people reject Jesus?"	Daniel 12:10; 1 Corinthians 2:14; 2 Peter 2:16-18
"What about all the hypocrites?"	Job 8:13; Matthew 7:1; Romans 14:12
"If a person is doing the best he can, God will accept him. Sincerity is what counts."	John 3:18,36; Romans 3:23; Romans 6:23; Hebrews 2:3
"Surely there is more than one way."	John 11:25; John 14:6
"There is too much to give up."	Psalm 116:12; Mark 8:36; Luke 18:29-30
"I will probably become a Christian someday."	Proverbs 27:1; Isaiah 55:6; Matthew 24:44; 2 Corinthians 6:2
"There are so many things in the Bible I can't understand," or "I must wait until I understand more."	Deuteronomy 29:29; Romans 11:33; 1 Corinthians 2:14; 1 Corinthians 13:12
"I'm really not such a bad person."	Genesis 6:5; 1 Kings 8:46; Proverbs 20:9; Isaiah 53:6; Isaiah 64:6; Romans 3:23; Galatians 3:22; 1 John 1:8
"Maybe we'll get another chance after we die."	Luke 16:19-31; Hebrews 9:27
"I'm too sinful to be saved. God won't accept me."	Mark 2:17; Romans 5:8; 1 Timothy 1:15

21. Humility. Humility. Humility. It can't be said enough. If you can't humbly imagine what you'd be like if Christ hadn't saved you, then you won't naturally possess a humble attitude toward those who don't believe. And that's too bad. Without Christ, there are no Disciples, and we are no different than anyone else—even the worst of sinners. Read Colossians 4:5-6. From these verses, infer how you can make sure that you don't turn people *away* from God rather than toward Him.

SUMMARY

Write a summary of this chapter.

CHAPTER 4

BECOMING A DISCIPLER

Are we there yet? How much farther? You've seen God change your life. You've seen God turn the hearts of your friends to Him. But there's still so far to go. Why does Discipleship take so long?

Sometimes we want to rush Discipleship—our own and that of others. Resist that urge. There are no shortcuts. Begging and nagging your Father won't get you (or others) to "Grandma's house" (metaphorically speaking) any faster.

If you want to be a Discipler, you need to keep this in mind: God isn't finished working in your life, and He isn't finished working in the lives of other Christians you know—especially those who have just decided to follow Christ.

The best thing you can do is be patient with yourself and others. (Note: Read Philippians 1:6 if you need a bit of encouragement.) Start or join a Discipleship small group with your Christ-following friends, pray together, go to church together—just make sure you give each other room to breathe and grow. Above all, be humble. Christ Discipled twelve people, all of whom ditched Him just when He needed them the most. Don't be surprised if Discipling others is harder than it seems. Don't be shocked if you mess up royally. Luckily for us, God is gracious and sovereign. He started a good thing in us, and He promises to see it through to the end. If we keep our eyes fixed on Jesus, we'll make it to "Grandma's house" in the end.

FOLLOW UP

1. It's a privilege to talk to people about Christ, to watch their eyes light up as they begin to realize just how much God loves them. There's an amazing excitement and high that goes along with deciding to follow Christ. But that's not where the story ends—that's just where it begins. As you read in *The Life*, the first book in this series, a Journey with God is a marathon. Read 1 Thessalonians 2:7-12. Did Paul:

    a. Ditch people once they accepted Christ?
    b. Think others would help them grow in their faith?
    c. Give them a book and tell them to "read up"?
    d. Encourage them by example to live lives worthy of God?

2. Again, think about 1 Thessalonians 2:7-12. What practical advice can you take with you from Paul's example? (You might also want to check out Acts 18:11.)

3. Next, take a look at Matthew 28:19. Jesus didn't just instruct His Disciples to tell others about Him; He told them to make more Disciples. Is this an important distinction? Why or why not?

4. Read 1 Corinthians 4:15.

    a. Why do you think Paul felt so personally responsible for the Corinthians, the people he had first taught about Jesus?

    b. Do you think people will always have such strong feelings for those whom they Disciple? If not, why do you think they might not?

5. Every person has value to God. Every person is in some way at the "center" of God's attention. Read Matthew 10:29-31. How does this view compare to your own view of others?

A HEART TO HELP OTHER DISCIPLES

6. You've read about Paul's commitment to help those who had recently accepted Christ as their Master. Look up the following verses about another major, yet often overlooked, component of helping others walk with God. Write a short paragraph explaining

why you personally believe this component is or isn't an integral part of Discipleship (Colossians 1:9-12; Colossians 4:12; 1 Thessalonians 1:3; 2 Timothy 1:3-4).

7. Look at your own life. Did you become a perfect Disciple overnight? Of course not. Nobody does, and if you Disciple others, they won't either. But how can you encourage a new believer to walk with Christ? What sort of things would you recommend to a person who has just decided to follow Christ? List four or five ideas. Here's one idea for starters:

- Make time every day to read God's Word.

-

-

-

-

8. You can do all the right things and encourage others to do all the right things, but even more important is your *reason* for doing it all. List some reasons why you as a Disciple do studies like this one, read the Bible, or pray. Put a star next to the number one reason you come up with.

9. As a follow-up to the last question, read Matthew 7:21-23. In this passage, Jesus talked about a group of people who supposedly had done all the right things—they had even performed miracles in God's name.

a. What happened to these people?

b. Verse 21 says that those who do the will of the Father will go to heaven. Why, then, were these people, who appeared to have had good behavior, rejected?

c. Figure this out. What does this say about doing God's will? (It obviously isn't as simple as "just doing it.")

d. How can you ensure that you and other Disciples won't end up like this group of people?

VALUES: CONTINUING OUR OWN DISCIPLESHIP

10. If you want to help others become Disciples, it's essential that you continue your own Discipleship. Paul understood this principle.

a. Infer why Paul was so confident in the example he set for others (Philippians 4:9).

b. Are you confident in the example you set? Why or why not?

c. What do you need to do to be a solid example for others to follow?

11. It's easy to get carried away with what the culture around us holds in high esteem. Money, sex, leisure . . . the world offers quite a few things that occupy the attention of our unsuspecting souls. As we make Disciples and continue our own Discipleship process, we need to stay focused on the goal, on what is most valuable. To what extent do you agree or disagree with Jesus' thoughts about what is most valuable (Luke 9:25)?

12. Flip forward a few pages to Luke 16:1-15. Again, Jesus told a story about what should be most valuable to a Disciple. Read this passage.

a. Does it seem strange to you that this dishonest person was commended by his master? Explain.

b. Why can't people serve both God and money?

c. Focus on the last verse, Jesus' response to the religious phonies of His day. Rewrite it in your own words.

d. How can you avoid being a religious hypocrite?

13. God's ways and values are far beyond our natural comprehension. That's one reason people resort to religiosity instead of a genuine relationship with God. In the DFD 2.0 series, much has been said, implicitly and explicitly, about adopting God's values and doing it with the only real motive. But if Isaiah 55:8-9 is true, how can a Disciple ever learn to think like God, to value what He values? (If you need a hint or just want to cheat, read Psalm 119:33-37.)

14. God's Spirit will help us understand, interpret, and apply God's Word. What is a Disciple's role in helping another believer get to that point (2 Timothy 2:15)?

15. There's a reason Jesus said, "Don't look for shortcuts to God" (Matthew 7:13, MSG). Being in a relationship with God requires our complete attention, our whole being: body, soul, and mind. By now you've almost finished this Bible study series. You'll probably go on to another one. Then another. Why? Why not take a shortcut? Why is this relationship worth such a commitment? Answer this question personally and honestly.

ALL WE NEED IS . . .

16. Hopefully the DFD 2.0 series has helped you realize that there is no secret formula to being in a relationship with God. We can study the Bible, pray, and tell others about Christ, but ultimately we love God because He first loved us and has called us to be His children. Because of this, we are free to love God and others. Read 1 John 4:10-12.

    a. According to verse 10, what is love?

    b. Why is it (or isn't it) important that God loved us first instead of the other way around? (Need help? See verse 10.)

c. If there were a "secret formula" to Christianity, it just might be love. What happens when Disciples live a life of love?

17. What connection is there between love of God and obedience to Him (1 John 5:3-5)?

17.5. In case you missed it the first time, *What connection is there between love of God and obedience to Him (1 John 5:3-5)?* This is a *major* part of being a Disciple. Please give it some thought.

18. In our Discipleship, there will be times of doubt, times when we won't *feel* like Disciples. How can we know that we really are God's children—that the Father hears us and that the Spirit is with us (1 John 3:19-24)?

19. In his poem, "The Second Coming," William Butler Yeats wrote, "Things fall apart." Thanks to sin, that's exactly right. Everything in

this world falls apart, *except* God and His kingdom. Make your life matter by treasuring Christ above everything in this world—TV, drugs, friends, accolades, comfort, and anything else people use to replace God in their lives. Read 1 John 2:15-17. Will a life of love and Discipleship fall apart? Why or why not?

SUMMARY

Congratulations! You finished.

Write one last summary. This time, summarize what it means to you personally to be a Disciple.